Animal Rights

DEBATING THE ISSUES

Animal Rights

GAIL MACK

Cavendish Square

Published by Cavendish Square Publishing, LLC

Website: www.cavendishsq.com

This publication represents the opinions and views of the author based on Gail Mack's personal experience, knowledge, and research. The information in this book serves as a general guide only. The author and publisher have used their best efforts in preparing this book and disclaim liability rising directly and indirectly from the use and application of this book.

All websites were available and accurate when this book was sent to press.

Library of Congress Cataloging-in-Publication Data

Mack, Gail.
Animal rights / Gail Mack. — 1st ed.
p. cm. — (Debating the issues)
Includes bibliographical references and index.
ISBN 978-0-7614-4967-6 (print) —ISBN 978-1-60870-662-4 (ebook)
1. Animal rights—Juvenile literature. I. Title. II. Series.
HV4708.M323 2012
179'.3—dc22
2010039298

Editor: Peter Mavrikis
Publisher: Michelle Bisson
Art Director: Anahid Hamparian
Series design by Sonia Chaghatzbanian

Photo research by Alison Morretta

Front cover: IndexStock/Superstock.
Associated Press: Jennifer DeMonte/Daily Inter Lake, 8; Joe Jaszewski/The Idaho Statesman, 9; April L. Brown, 17; Associated Press, 21, 28; Susan Ragan, 27; John Dearing/Bureau of Land Management, 30; Steve Parsons, 32; Ted S. Warren, 36; Busch Gardens, Tampa Bay/Press Association, 37; Marcio Jose Sanchez, 40; Gary Kazanjian, 43. ***Bridgeman Art Library***: The Bridgeman Art Library International, 12. ***Getty Images***: altrendo images, 6; Mark S. Wexler, 11; Melanie Stetson Freeman/The Christian Science Monitor, 16; Kim Steele, 19; Daniel J. Cox, 32; Bill Pugliano, 35; Stephane De Sakutin/AFP, 47; Alberto Simon/AFP, 50; Chris Hondros, 57. ***Superstock***: Frances M. Roberts/Ambient Images, 1, 2-3, 4-5; image100, 14; age fotostock, 24; IndexStock, 52, 54.
Back cover: age fotostock/Superstock.

Printed in the United States of America
135642

Table of Contents

Chapter 1

LIVING TOGETHER

From the earliest times, humans have relied on animals to perform many kinds of jobs. Dogs help people with disabilities. They are trained to guide people who cannot see and to alert the hearing impaired when someone knocks at the door, rings the doorbell, or calls on the phone. Dogs often work as partners with police officers. These dogs are trained to sniff out drugs and explosives and to track criminals. Working dogs living on farms and ranches herd sheep and cattle. Some breeds serve as watchdogs for property owners and businesses. Cats also work. On farms, for instance, they are used to keep barns free of mice.

Humans have also used animals for clothing. Sheep and alpacas provide wool. Minks, rabbits, and other fur-bearing animals are killed for their pelts. Leather is made from the hides of cattle and other animals—even crocodiles. Today there are alternatives to using animal fur and skins. Many fabrics are woven from plants such as cotton and flax.

Humans' Best Friends

Dogs have lived with humans for more than 14,000 years. It is believed that prehistoric humans first used them as watchdogs and later

A seeing-eye dog guides his blind owner as they walk along a city sidewalk.

A furry barn cat ignores the antics of its stable pal.

put them to work herding and hunting other animals. The more than four hundred breeds of dogs that exist today have shown their intelligence, loyalty, companionship, and abilities in many different ways. Their services include tracking criminals, finding lost persons, sniffing out illegal drugs and explosives, serving as "eyes" for the blind and "ears" for the deaf, as well as helping others with a variety of tasks. So-called therapy dogs are used to cheer up patients in hospitals and nursing homes. Having a dog as a loyal companion may provide health benefits. Petting a dog, for example, can slow the heart rate and lower blood pressure.

Cats are smart and independent. Like dogs, they can be playful and entertaining, and, like dogs, domestic cats have jobs to do. Cats can see better in darkness than people can. They climb trees, have an amazing sense of balance, and can walk along narrow ledges or fences. They are speedy runners and can leap long distances. When they fall, they almost always land on their feet. These abilities make them skillful hunters, especially of mice, rats, and snakes. Although a cornered cat can be dangerous—it will hiss and scratch with its sharp claws—cats can also be loving and very patient with little children.

Cats, with their big, glowing eyes, seem mysterious creatures to many people. The ancient Egyptians believed cats were sacred and protected their homes. Because of their beauty and grace, cats have been painted and drawn by many artists throughout the centuries.

Twins Julia and Claire have a sensory muscular disorder, but they have a great time with Ovelle, a six-year-old Labrador retriever, during feeding therapy at St. Alphonsus Rehabilitation in Meridian, Ohio.

The Original Horsepowered Engine

Horses, as well as oxen and mules, have been used as beasts of burden—animals that carry heavy packs of tools and supplies and pull plows, wagons, and carriages. Horses have been hardworking partners and friends of humans for many years, although in the beginning, early humans most likely hunted horses for food. However, when people realized how fast and powerful horses are, they learned to ride them to hunt other animals. Horses have done—and still do—a great variety of jobs.

Horses are especially remembered for their role in delivering the mail to settlers in the expanding Old West in the nineteenth century. The Pony Express, an overland mail service that operated from April 1860 to November 1861, carried mail between Saint Joseph, Missouri, and Sacramento, California. The journey, which took, on average, ten days, required making regular stops at a network of relay stations along the 2,000-mile (3,220-kilometer) route for the rider to get a fresh mount. Among the riders were William F. Cody (who would later become known as Buffalo Bill) and "Pony Bob" Haslam. The Pony Express ended when the transcontinental telegraph system was completed.

DID YOU KNOW?

In 1861, a wounded Pony Express rider named "Pony Bob" Haslam rode 120 miles (190 km) from a station at the foot of Lake Tahoe, in the mountains between California and Nevada, to a station near Fort Churchill, 75 miles (120 km) to the east, in eight hours and twenty minutes. His shipment included President Abraham Lincoln's inaugural address.

An Amish farmer and his five horses work together to pull a plow through his field.

From the thirteenth to the eighteenth century, laws that discouraged acts of cruelty to animals were in effect. However, these laws did not prohibit animal entertainments such as **bearbaiting**, cockfighting, and horse racing or fishing, hawking, and hunting.

In England, the Sunday Observance Act was passed in 1625 under the rule of King Charles I. This law prohibited meetings, assemblies, sports, and pastimes such as bull- and bearbaiting on Sundays. Two years later, other prohibited Sunday activities were added to this bill, including travel by horse-drawn carriages and wagons, cattle driving, and the killing of animals by butchers. In 1664, under Charles II,

KING ASHOKA

In the third century BCE, Ashoka, king of the Mauryan Empire of India, established laws that protected animals. Today animal rights **activists** honor him not only for creating the first list of "protected" **species** but also for declaring what many modern-day activists believe—that animals must not be slaughtered either for food or for sacrifice.

Ashoka reigned from about 269 to 232 BCE. At first, he was a fierce warrior who led many military conquests. After his conquest of the country of Kalinga, on India's eastern coast, he was affected by the suffering the war had caused and renounced armed conquest. At this time, he adopted Buddhism. His teachings, called edicts, were carved into rocks and stone pillars.

Ashoka practiced many of the virtues he taught, including **compassion**, honesty, truthfulness, and nonviolence to people and animals. He toured rural areas of India to preach the Buddhist "right way of life" (called dharma) and to help relieve the sufferings of the poor.

Ashoka did much to create a peaceful and just society that included compassion for animals. He built hospitals for animals as well as for people. He banned the hunting of certain species and discouraged cruelty to domestic and wild animals. He also advocated a vegetarian diet.

Detail of a pillar with an engraved edict.

a law was passed that carried the death penalty for those who set fire to property and crops or hurt or killed horses, sheep, or cattle.

DID YOU KNOW?

In 1641, the Massachusetts Colony Body of Liberties passed a law that compelled those driving cattle long distances to stop and rest animals that were weary, hungry, or sick.

In the 1700s, laws were passed that forbade cattle drives through the cities of London and Westminster. Cattle drivers who mistreated the animals during the drives in the countryside were fined or sent to prison.

WHAT DO YOU THINK?

How did people in earlier times abuse or mistreat animals?

Why did King Charles I and II make laws that stopped animal abuse on Sundays?

Do you think animals communicate with people? If you do, how do you think they do it?

If you were making a list of rights for animals, what rights would you include?

Chapter 2

Many people do not believe that animals need or deserve legal rights. Their belief is based on their opinion that animals are not enough like humans. For example, do animals feel emotions? Human emotions include love, fear, joy, sadness, surprise, anxiety, and anger. People who believe that animals cannot feel emotions do not think that they are entitled to legal rights. Although people often see human qualities in animals, regular scientific methods cannot prove that animals feel emotions.

Many people believe that animals merely act—and react—according to their instincts, and that they lack any ability to think and reason.

Animal Agriculture: Keeping Animals Healthy

Americans spend about $142 billion a year on beef, chicken, pork, turkey, and lamb and eat, on average, about 200 pounds (90 kilograms) of meat, poultry, and fish per person per year. Nearly 10 billion animals are killed each year. In 2002, the U.S. Department of Agriculture's Natural Resources Conservation Service reported that there were nearly 2 billion farms and ranches in the United States.

A shopper at a supermarket selects a package of meat.

The National Association of State Departments of Agriculture (NASDA) was founded in 1915. The NASDA's mission is to ensure the well-being of animals. Its work includes developing ways to protect animals from disease-causing germs, called pathogens, so that the germs do not enter the food chain. Because there is not enough science-based information on what produces a state of well-being in animals, NASDA members also study ways to improve management practices and systems that will improve animals' well-being. The NASDA develops public policy and programs that support and promote the American agricultural industry while protecting consumers and the environment.

THE ANIMAL AND PLANT HEALTH INSPECTION SERVICE

The Animal and Plant Health Inspection Service (APHIS) is a division of the Department of Agriculture. It works to protect and improve the health, quality, and marketability of the nation's animals (including various wildlife), animal products, and medicinal veterinary products, such as vaccines. The APHIS also provides overviews of domestic animal health in the United States, as well as of the programs and strategies used to ensure the animals' continued health.

The APHIS also includes the Office of the Chief Information

A quality assurance manager at a restaurant chain shucks, or opens, an oyster in order to test it.

Officer of Veterinary Services. This office provides information technology services and delivery to Veterinary Services (VS). The APHIS also moves quickly to enforce penalties in response to animal welfare violations, including violations of the Animal Welfare Act (AWA) and the Horse Protection Act (HPA).

ANIMAL AGRICULTURE ALLIANCE

Animal agriculture is essential to preserving America's security and vitality. The mission of the Animal Agriculture Alliance (established in 1987) is to talk about the importance of modern animal agriculture to consumers and the media. Using science-based research, the alliance dispenses information on topics ranging from animal welfare to biotechnology. The alliance also explains how America's farmers and ranchers produce the safest and most affordable food in the world while maintaining high standards of animal well-being.

Chickens gather around their feeders in a poultry house in rural Washington County, Arkansas.

ANTIBIOTICS

Antibiotics are an important tool that farmers and ranchers use to ensure that their animals are both healthy and productive. The Animal Agriculture Alliance supports the responsible use of antibiotics by producers. In order to provide the American consumer with a high-quality source of protein, farmers and ranchers follow herd and flock health-management programs designed to keep their animals healthy. Antibiotics must go through a complicated, difficult approval process before being approved by the U.S. Food and Drug Administration (FDA). Many farmers, veterinarians, and lawmakers agree that these medicines help producers provide safe, affordable food.

CALIFORNIA'S EARLY-WARNING SYSTEM

California protects both livestock and consumers with the California Animal Health and Food Safety (CAHFS) Laboratory System, which is responsible for making swift diagnoses of animal diseases affecting humans. It partners with California's Department of Food and Agriculture at the Davis campus of the University of California and with veterinarians and livestock and poultry producers.

Medical Testing Using Animals

Animals are used for medical testing because it is necessary and benefits humans. The goal is to experiment with new medicines and vaccines first on animals to see how the medicines affect them before doing human studies. Throughout the world about 50 million to

These caged rabbits are used as test subjects for antibody production in a research facility in India.

100 million vertebrate animals, from zebra fish to monkeys, chimpanzees, and other vertebrates, are used in experiments every year. Mice, rats, birds, fish, frogs and other animals, however, are not included in this figure. Some 80 million mice and rats were used in experiments in the United States in 2001. Animals used in experiments are usually **euthanized** afterward. There are several sources of research animals. Most are bred for use in experiments; others are caught in the wild or bought from dealers who get them at auctions or from animal pounds.

Different countries regulate the use of animals in different ways. Those that support using animals for experiments argue that nearly every twentieth-century medical achievement used animals in various

Where Is Testing Done and for What Kinds of Research Are Animals Used?

WHERE	KINDS OF RESEARCH	OTHER
Universities and medical schools	Biomedical	Education
Defense contractor laboratories	Genetics	Breeding
Pharmaceutical companies	Behavioral studies	Defense research
Commercial laboratories and other facilities	Developmental biology	
Farms	Xenotransplantation	
	Drug testing	
	Toxicology	
	Cosmetics testing	

ways. Supporters of animal use insist that computers cannot model the ways in which different things might interact during a test.

Victory over Polio

In 1921, outbreaks of polio (poliomyelitis) swept through the United States. Polio, an infectious viral disease, has been around since ancient times. Polio attacks the nerve cells and sometimes the central nervous system and usually causes paralysis and sometimes even death. Its early symptoms are like those of the flu. Polio strikes mostly children, but adults can also be infected. Polio struck Franklin D. Roosevelt (who later became a U.S. president) just a few days after he had gone swimming during a family vacation in 1921. Roosevelt thought he had developed a cold—but it was polio. His legs were left permanently paralyzed.

In the 1940s, Dr. Jonas Salk used rhesus monkey **cross-contamination** studies to isolate the three forms of the poliovirus that affected hundreds of thousands yearly. Salk's team created a vaccine against the strains of polio in cultures of monkey kidney cells. In 1952, the United States suffered an outbreak of 58,000 polio cases, and in the following year 35,000 cases. The Salk vaccine, which used dead viruses, was made publicly available in 1955 and reduced the number of polio cases fifteenfold in the United States over the following five years. Dr. Albert Sabin made a superior "live" vaccine by passing the poliovirus through animal hosts, including monkeys. His oral vaccine (the doses are taken by mouth) was produced

In the 1950s, Dr. Jonas Salk, first to develop a polio vaccine, holds aloft bottles containing a culture used to grow the vaccine.

DID YOU KNOW?

Mold, a woolly growth, usually fungal in origin, often appears in damp areas or on foods. In 1928, Alexander Fleming, a British scientist, noticed mold growing on a germ-culture medium. The mold, *Penicillium notatum*, had ruined the culture. Ten years later, scientists isolated an antibacterial molecule in the mold, which they named penicillin. Since then, many different forms of penicillin have been developed to treat a wide range of diseases.

for public use in 1963 and is still in use. It had virtually stamped out polio in the United States by 1965. An estimated 100,000 rhesus monkeys were killed in the course of developing the polio vaccines; sixty-five doses of vaccine were produced from each monkey. The two vaccines have wiped out polio in most countries throughout the world. The worldwide number of cases dropped from about 350,000 cases in 1988 to 1,652 cases in 2008.

SARS

SARS (severe acute respiratory syndrome) is an illness that affects the lungs and breathing and can lead to pneumonia. It is caused by a SARS-related **coronavirus** (SARS-CoV). The first outbreak was reported in Asia in February 2003. Over the next few months, SARS spread to more than two dozen countries in North America, South America, Europe, and Asia before it was contained.

The World Health Organization (WHO) has reported that 8,098 people worldwide became sick with SARS in the 2003 outbreak. Of these, 774 died. In the United States, only eight people caught the infection—all had traveled and been exposed to the SARS virus in other parts of the world. The disease did not spread widely in the United States.

SARS seems to spread mainly through close contact: hugging, kissing, sharing eating or drinking utensils, touching someone, or talking to someone a few feet away or closer. You cannot catch it just from walking past someone or sitting across from someone in a large waiting room or office.

SYMPTOMS OF SARS

Generally, SARS begins with high fever—that is, a temperature higher than 100.4 degrees Fahrenheit (38.0 degrees Centigrade). Fever is followed by

- mild respiratory symptoms
- headache
- overall feeling of discomfort
- body aches
- diarrhea (10 to 20 percent of patients)
- dry cough (after two to seven days)
- pneumonia

The SARS virus hitches a ride on droplets that spread when an infected person sneezes or coughs. Droplets can fly about 3 feet (1 meter) through the air and land on or in the **mucous membranes** of a nearby person's mouth, nose, or eyes. A person may also catch the disease by touching a surface or object that contains the infectious droplets and then touching his or her nose, mouth, or eyes. The virus may also spread by other yet unknown ways.

Researchers found that a new coronavirus never seen in humans was the cause of SARS. In experiments at a medical center in Rotterdam, the Netherlands, researchers infected monkeys with the new coronavirus. The monkeys developed a lung disease exactly the same as SARS.

Ultimately, a SARS vaccine was developed. A federal health agency, the Centers for Disease Control (CDC), was, as of 2011, continuing to work with other federal agencies, state and local health

DID YOU KNOW?

More than 95 percent of the SARS cases took place in twelve countries or areas in the World Health Organization's Western Pacific Region.

departments, and other health-care organizations to plan for rapid recognition of and response to the disease should it ever come back.

Protections for Lab Animals

Today in the United States, researchers must follow certain laws and regulations, both federal and state. A federal law, the Animal Welfare Act of 1966, requires adequate food and shelter for certain kinds of lab animals. The National Institutes of Health, a federal agency, requires each institution it funds to establish a committee to oversee the use and care of the animals.

In the United States, scientists experiment on more than 20 million animals a year, although animal rights advocates estimate that as many as 100 million animals—90 percent of which are mice and rats—are used as subjects in biological, medical, and psychological studies. In addition to mice and rats, researchers also use birds, cats, dogs, guinea pigs, hamsters, monkeys and other primates, and rabbits. Educators use animals to teach students anatomy, physiology, biology, and surgery.

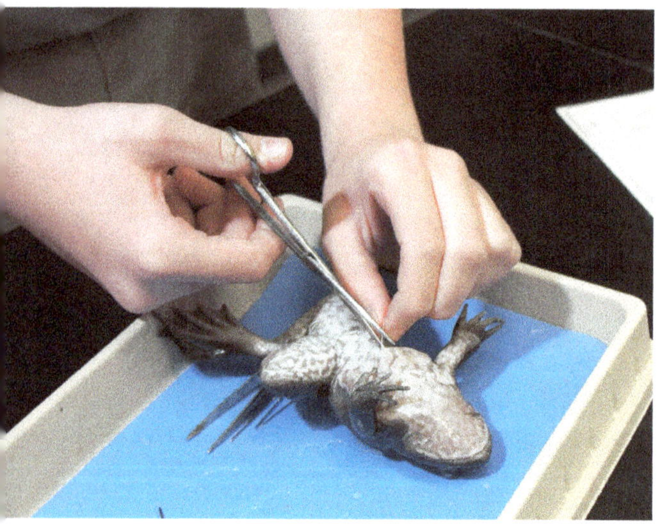

A student dissects a frog in biology class.

Medical researchers study animals to learn about their body processes and how they relate to those of humans. Researchers also use animals to learn about the causes and effects of cancer, heart disease, and other illnesses. In addition, they use animals to develop and test drugs, surgical methods, and safety standards in cosmetic and food products. Psychologists conduct experiments to study the effects of stress, such as hunger, to learn how these conditions affect humans.

Xenotransplantation

A patient waiting for a healthy organ to replace a faulty one—a heart, a kidney, or a pancreas, for example—could have a long wait. More than 100,000 people are on waiting lists to receive an organ donation, but fewer than 30,000 transplants were performed in 2008. Most people on the waiting list are waiting for new kidneys.

As a result, people are looking more and more at the possibilities of transplants using organs, tissues, and cells from nonhuman animals. On October 6, 2009, in a **clinical trial** held at Middlemore Hospital, in Auckland, New Zealand, researchers injected the cells from an Auckland Island piglet pancreas into the abdomen of a forty-eight-year-old man who had had type 1 diabetes for twenty years. In type 1 diabetes, the body mistakenly attacks and destroys insulin-producing cells in the pancreas. Diabetes can cause blindness and poor blood circulation, a condition that could lead to limb amputation. A company executive admits that the treatment will not eliminate all symptoms but notes that the piglets are of a type recovered from 150 years of isolation on islands south of New Zealand and carry no known virus or germ that could infect humans.

Within two months, the patient had cut down his daily insulin injections by 30 percent. The pig cells are coated in a seaweed-based gel and release the hormone insulin (which is needed for the metabolism of carbohydrates and the regulation of blood sugar) and other essential hormones. The pig insulin is very similar to human insulin. The clinical trial at Middlemore followed trials at lower-dosage rates of the **Diabecell implants** in Russia, where a woman went off insulin completely.

Americans for Medical Progress (AMP) is a nonprofit charity organization supported by universities, private research facilities, research-related businesses, and scientific and professional societies. It is also funded by foundation grants and contributions from individuals.

The AMP board of directors includes researchers, veterinarians, physicians, university officials, and two Nobel laureates in medicine. The first human kidney transplant was performed by Dr. Joseph Murray, one of the two Nobel Prize winners, in 1954. In 1996, Dr. Murray wrote a column in the *Los Angeles Times* about a patient named Jeff Getty. In 1995, Getty, who was under treatment for cancer and AIDS, received an experimental bone marrow transplant from a baboon. Doctors hoped that the baboon's bone marrow would help develop cells that would fight AIDS but not get the disease. Getty was the first person to receive a bone marrow transplant from one species to another, a procedure called **xenotransplantation**. Getty's doctors hoped to create two immune systems that would work side by side—the human's and the baboon's. Getty's health improved, but because the baboon's bone marrow quickly disappeared from his system, doctors concluded that it was not the reason for his improvement. Getty died in 2006 of heart failure at the age of forty-nine.

Animal activists viewed the experiment as morally wrong because the baboon donor was killed. It had been **anesthetized** during the removal of its cells and was euthanized because its tissues were to be used in further research. In his column, Dr. Murray wrote:

AIDS patient Jeff Getty, 38, waves as he leaves San Francisco's General Hospital on January 4, 1996, less than a month after he received a bone marrow transplant from a baboon.

> [a]nimal activists oppose all animal-based medical research. If we had listened to their arguments 50 years ago, children still would be contracting polio (the vaccine was developed in monkeys). Diabetics would not have insulin, a benefit of research on dogs. We would also be without antibiotics for pneumonia, chemotherapy for cancer, surgery for heart diseases, organ transplants and joint replacement.

Animals in Outer Space

A Russian dog named Laika was the first living creature in space. In Russian, *laika* means "howler," or "barker." The Russian experiment with Laika was a very important step. It paved the way for humans to make their first explorations of outer space. On November 3, 1957, Laika flew into space aboard *Sputnik 2*, a 250-pound (113-kg) Soviet satellite. The dog rode in a cabin equipped with a television camera and devices that measured her temperature and her blood pressure. Among the devices were a radio transmitter and an instrument that measured **ultraviolet radiation** and **X-ray radiation**. The space capsule reached speeds of nearly 18,000 miles per hour (28,800 km/h). The experiment proved that a living passenger could survive being launched into orbit and endure weightlessness. It showed that human spaceflight would be possible, and it provided scientists with some of the first data on how living organisms react to spaceflight environments. The satellite continued circling Earth until April 14, 1958. It made 2,570 orbits before it reentered Earth's atmosphere.

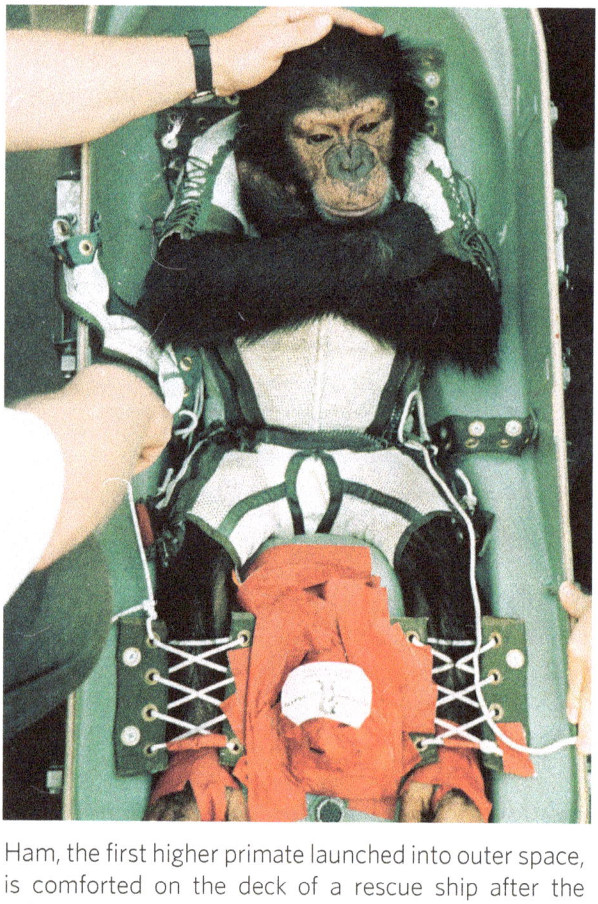

Ham, the first higher primate launched into outer space, is comforted on the deck of a rescue ship after the splashdown on January 31, 1961, of the Project Mercury capsule in which he rode.

HAM AND ENOS: CHIMPS IN SPACE

In the early days of the U.S. space program, chimpanzees were aboard early missions before humans headed for the moon. Two chimpanzees in particular helped the astronauts to learn more about outer space:

Ham zoomed into space before the first American, Alan Shepherd, flew into the unknown, and Enos flew just before John Glenn orbited Earth.

Ham and Enos were two of a group of chimps that the U.S. Air Force trained to test the physical effects of launch and spaceflight, including weightlessness, cosmic radiation, and high acceleration.

ARABELLA AND ANITA: SPIDERS IN SPACE

Arabella and Anita, two female cross spiders were the first Australian animals in space—and the first eight-legged creatures to make a space trip. They traveled to the *Skylab 3* space station. A student from Lexington, Virginia, Judy Miles, had suggested an experiment to see if spiders could spin webs in near-weightless conditions.

On her first day in orbit, Arabella, a little unsteady, at first seemed to be making irregular swimming motions. Then still not quite adjusted to the weightlessness, she spun a rather sloppy web. Soon she was spinning webs just like the ones she made on land. The silk was finer than that spun on land and was thick in some places and thin in others. Aboard *Skylab 3*, the spiders were given some juicy steak and a water-soaked sponge. Eventually, they died and their bodies are now at the Smithsonian Museum in Washington, D.C., in memory of their part in helping humans learn about the effects of life in space.

Animal Rights Activists as Terrorists

In April 2009, the Federal Bureau of Investigation (FBI) named a thirty-one-year-old American animal rights activist to its list of "most wanted

ATF agents sift through ashes at the site of a fire at the Bureau of Land Management's horse facility near Reno, Nevada, in 2001. The radical group Earth Liberation Front (ELF) claimed responsibility for the fire.

terrorists." The FBI said the man was a "domestic terrorist" and "should be considered armed and dangerous." According to the FBI, the man may have been involved in the bombings of two San Francisco–area office buildings.

In 2005, the FBI and the Bureau of Alcohol, Tobacco, Firearms and Explosives (ATF) were concerned with both the animal rights group Animal Liberation Front and the ecoterrorist group Earth Liberation Front (ELF). Officials from the FBI and ATF said animal and environmental rights extremists had claimed credit for more than 1,200 criminal incidents since 1990. In 2005, the FBI had 150 pending investigations associated with the two groups.

Animals in Entertainment

People need recreation to balance their lives. Studies have shown that not only individuals but society as a whole benefits from recreation. Zoos are an important and hugely popular source of recreation for people all over the world. In America, the Association of Zoos and Aquariums (AZA) reports that every year 150 million people visit AZA-accredited zoos and aquariums.

DID YOU KNOW?

The Central Park Zoo, in New York City, was the first zoo in America. It opened in 1864.

WHAT DO YOU THINK?

Does experimentation on animals serve a worthwhile purpose? Why or why not?

If people did not use animals for experimentation, what research options might they have?

Why can pigs' organs be used for transplants in humans?

Is the use of violence to ensure that animal rights are protected justified?

If you could make laws for animal protection, what laws would you make?

Chapter 3

How do humans show sadness or happiness, anger or fear? How do animals show the same emotions? Dog and cat owners can usually tell when their animals feel happy or sad, full of joy or fear. Researchers who study animal minds have found that animals, like humans, feel—and display—emotions.

The field of animal emotions is a part of the larger science called **cognitive ethology** (the study of animal minds). Research in animal emotions has grown and changed a lot over the last thirty years. Today most people who once wondered or doubted whether animals really could have emotions have discovered that animals do indeed have many of the same kinds of emotions that humans have.

In their studies, researchers make a distinction between primary and secondary emotions. Primary emotions—there are six of them—are basic feelings that do not require conscious thought: they are like automatic reflexes. These six universal emotions were identified by Charles Darwin, who was the first scientist to study animal emotions systematically. In his book *The Expression of the Emotions in Man and Animals*, published in 1872, he wrote that animals could feel the primary emotions: fear, disgust, anger, surprise, sadness, and happiness.

Do animals have emotions? Two orangutans hug each other in Malaysia.

These emotions are produced in a part of the brain called the limbic system, which includes the amygdala. In 1952, a scientist named Paul MacLean called this part of the brain the "emotional" part. Humans and many other species have limbic systems. Other researchers have added to Darwin's list. In his book *A Natural History of Human Emotions*, Stuart Walton adds jealousy, contempt, shame, and embarrassment. Antonio Damasio, a neuroscientist, writing in *Descartes' Error*, added "social emotions": sympathy, guilt, pride, envy, admiration, and indignation. Marc Bekoff, a professor emeritus of ecology and evolutionary biology, notes in his 2007 book *The Emotional Lives of Animals*, "It's interesting that none of these researchers mention love."

Human-Animal Bonding

In earlier times, animals were domesticated so that humans could use them for various jobs: for example, dogs were herders and trackers, and cats patrolled barns and homes and hunted for rats and mice to kill. The animals usually were kept outside.

Today in Western societies, many dogs have important work to do. Some dogs, partnered with police officers, help catch criminals, control crowds, sniff out drugs and explosives, and search for people trapped by earthquakes, avalanches, and other disasters. Assistance dogs help disabled people in a number of ways: they pick up dropped objects and open doors, let their owners know when someone knocks at the door or calls on the phone, and guide them across busy streets or down onto subway platforms. Many shepherds still help ranchers and farmers protect and control their cattle and sheep.

Cats serve mostly as pets, but many live in barns or shops and do what they love—hunt and catch mice and rats.

Animals that are pets bond, or connect, with their owners and become as much a part of the family as its human members.

A Michigan police officer and his bomb-sniffing dog Spencer are on patrol at the Detroit Metropolitan Wayne County Airport.

In 1980, scientists at the University of Pennsylvania found that human-to-animal contact reduced stress and lowered blood pressure levels, heart rates, respiratory rates, anxiety, and tension. Today therapy animals bring joy to hospital patients; to old, often lonely, people in nursing homes; and to children with illnesses or disabilities, as well as providing companionship to their owners.

In the United States, 1.2 billion animals are kept as pets. Today, researchers continue to explore the ways in which both animals and humans can benefit from bonding.

Animals also develop lasting bonds with other animals, sometimes of their own species and sometimes of other species. For example, at

PARTNERS AND BUDDIES

In the 1800s in the Old West, sheriffs and marshalls patrolled their beats on horseback, covering long distances between towns. As towns grew into cities, mounted police units much like army cavalry divisions were formed to fight crime and keep the peace.

Back east, New York City was the first to establish a mounted police unit (1871). Many big cities now have mounted police units whose main job is crowd control. They work at parades, control angry crowds of striking workers, and calm noisy demonstrators. A police officer atop a powerful horse is not to be argued with. However, their jobs can be dangerous—angry people can hurt a horse and its rider by throwing things at them, or an out-of-control car could hit them.

Thoroughbreds, quarter horses, Tennessee walking horses, and huge Percherons and Clydesdales are some breeds that complete their training and join the mounted division. Police horses need to be brave, strong, cooperative, and obedient. Many have had previous careers in rodeos, racing, or horse shows. As police horses, they learn to trust their riders and to get used to traffic on busy streets. Those headed for big cities also learn to go through fire and what to do if they hear a gunshot.

Each horse is partnered with a police officer, who is responsible for grooming, feeding, and saddling the horse. On duty, they take breaks so that the horse can have water, hay, oats, and grass. As time goes by, the partners build a lasting bond of affection and trust.

U.S. Border Patrol Agents ride mustangs adopted from the U.S. Bureau of Land Management's wild horse and burro program.

What could these two possibly have in common? Perhaps their long, skinny necks. Bea, the giraffe, and Wilma, an ostrich, have become the best of friends at Busch Gardens Tampa Bay's 65-acre Serengeti Plain.

a wildlife rescue center in England, a piglet and a dog became fast friends, and in the United States, a black cat formed a cuddling relationship with a neighbor's big dog.

DID YOU KNOW?

The Humane Society of the United States, based in Washington, D.C., is the largest animal advocacy organization in the world. In 2010, it had 11 million members and a budget of $120 million.

Factory Farming

In 1975, an Australian named Peter Singer called attention to the abuse of animals throughout the world in a book titled *Animal Liberation*. In the book, Singer, a philosopher and a professor at Princeton University, described the plight of helpless chickens, pigs, and other animals housed in what Singer called factory farms. Chickens were the first to be taken from old-fashioned farm environments and put into cages so small that they could not walk around, spread their wings, or scratch the ground.

For Singer, the issue is not animal rights but animal equality. He charges that humans are what he calls speciesists—creatures who put the interests of their own species above those of other species. He says that in the past, most people did not believe that animals could suffer. They also believed that animals had no interests and that humans, therefore, could not be guilty of neglecting their interests. Nor did people believe that animals have thoughts or feelings. Although Singer rejects the use of the word *rights,* his book sparked the animal rights movement. The most important reason to consider animals' interests, he says, is that, like humans, animals can and do suffer.

Factory farms, also called corporate farms, are big business. They can have thousands of animals. Livestock are kept in cages that are housed in buildings where air, heating, cooling, feeding, and watering are controlled automatically by high-tech machines. The animals are identified by numbers. There is much debate over factory farms: Food production may be efficient, but is there animal abuse? Are factory farms, with their huge output, necessary because of growing world population? How do they affect the environment—is animal waste polluting land and water? What are the health risks for humans and for the animals? International organizations such as the United Nations and the World Organization for Animal Health (OIE) say that only about forty out of two hundred countries are able to respond adequately to a health crisis stemming from swine flu, avian flu, West Nile virus, and other animal diseases.

Californians made history in 2008 when they approved Proposition 2, a landmark ballot initiative that bans three of the cruelest confinement systems used in factory farming. These are battery cages, veal crates, and gestation crates. Factory farms must comply with the new regulations by 2015. With this vote, California became the fifth state to ban gestation crates, the third to ban veal crates, and the first to ban battery cages.

The new law will not only lessen the suffering of millions of animals in California, it may also spark new laws against animal cruelty throughout the United States.

A battery cage is a cage the size of a filing drawer. Five or more hens are crammed into one cage. Each hen occupies a space the size of a piece of typing paper. The hens cannot touch the ground or extend their wings. The crowding often causes the birds to become aggressive, and they sometimes peck at and eat each other. To resolve this problem, some factory farms debeak the chickens. Hens living in these conditions produce 95 percent of the eggs in the United States. The new California law will require egg producers to give the hens—some 19 million animals—enough space to turn around comfortably and spread their wings.

A gestation crate is a metal enclosure that is a few feet wide and used to confine a pregnant sow. The sow can barely move, and it can-

More than 500,000 chickens at an egg processing plant were housed in battery cages that give chickens a space the size of a sheet of paper.

not do the things pigs usually do, such as root around in dirt. Pigs are very intelligent, and they love interesting activities. Without activity, like humans, they get bored and show signs of being unhappy. In modern factory farms, pigs are confined in small spaces that limit their movement. They are able only to stand up or lie down. Like the hens, they have no straw or other kinds of bedding materials because these would make cleaning difficult and time-consuming. Like the hens that develop "vices" such as pecking and eating each other, pigs also manifest abnormal behavior. They bite each other's tails and fight, and they do not gain enough weight to satisfy the farmers. The U.S. Department of Agriculture (USDA) recommends that the farmers cut off their tails, but it does not recommend using painkillers or anesthetics. Like the hens, many pigs die of stress.

A veal crate is used to confine calves destined to become veal. The calves live most of their lives inside these enclosures—which are about the same size as gestation crates—and are usually chained by the neck. The calves cannot turn around, stretch their legs, or lie down comfortably.

California voters shone a spotlight on these cruel practices and won publicity—television appearances and commercials that opened people's eyes throughout the country to these business operations.

Is Animal Agriculture Dangerous?

At a hearing of a House of Representatives subcommittee held on July 14, 2010, Dr. John Clifford, the USDA's deputy administrator of APHIS, admitted what many people in the United States—including officials of the FDA and CDC—had already concluded that the use of antibiotics in farm animal feed is contributing to the growing resistance to antibiotics in America.

The animal agriculture industry gives its hogs, chickens, and cattle a daily dose of antibiotics in their feed. The drugs help animals grow bigger, faster, and healthier. The bacteria are fighting back, however—they **mutate** and develop resistance to the antibiotics.

A Pew Charitable Trust report, "Human Health and Industrial Farming," notes that "industrial farms use antibiotics not only to treat sick animals, but also to offset crowding and poor sanitation, as well as to spur animal growth." According to the report, up to 70 percent of all antibiotics sold in the United States are given to healthy food animals.

In some cattle industry operations, growth hormone implants are used to increase calves' growth rate. Hormone use has stimulated much debate over the impact of eating meat with increased hormone levels. According to the organization Beyond Factory Farming, based in Canada, the human body uses only minute levels of hormones, and even the slightest changes in levels can result in serious physical problems. The European Union does not allow imports of meat from animals treated with hormones, including beef and pork from Canada. Many of the hormones used in the Canadian cattle industry are linked to various forms of cancer. In hog operations, reproductive and other kinds of hormones are used to control breeding cycles, and others are used to speed growth rates.

Another danger is disease. In 1986, mad cow disease was first recognized in cattle in the United Kingdom (UK). It grew into an epidemic there, especially in southern England, and cases were also reported in other parts of Europe and in Canada. This incurable disease takes two to five years to **incubate**. Its medical name is bovine spongiform encephalopathy (pronounced BO-vine SPUN-jih-form en-seh-fah-LA-puh-thee), or BSE. It causes the brain and spinal cord to break down and look much like sponges. Cattle become agitated and nervous, act strangely, and lose control of their ability to do normal things, such as walk. A cow that contracts BSE will die within a year. The disease appeared when the process used to make dietary supplements from

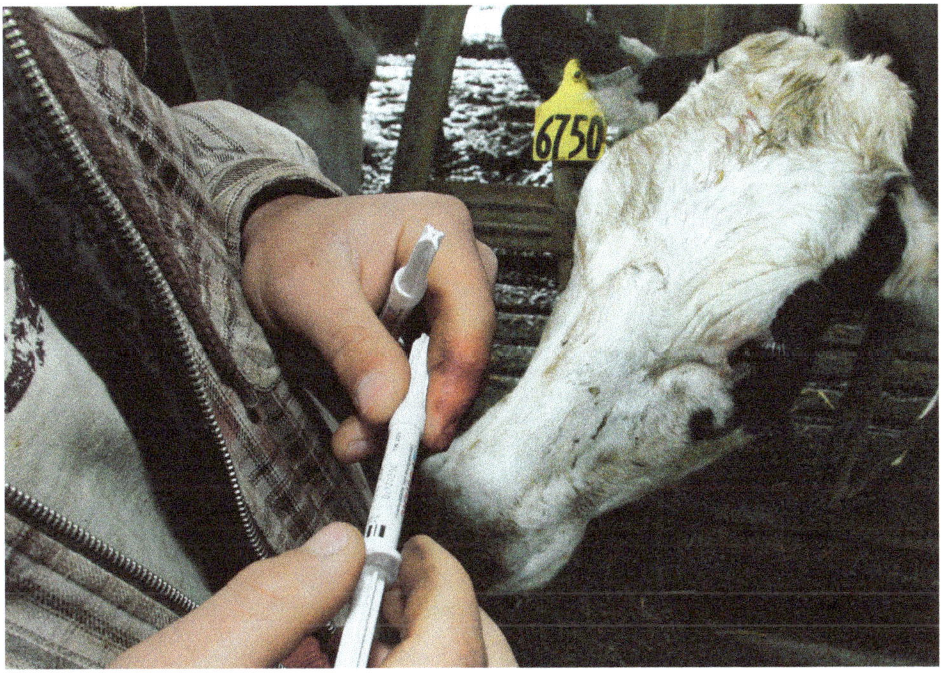

A worker at a California dairy holds vials of rBST, a bovine hormone, before he injects a cow.

animal remains was modified: temperatures were lowered and other ingredients were changed. These modifications allowed the infectious agent to revive and begin infecting animals. In 1988, the British government banned the use of animal-derived proteins in feed for cattle and other **ruminants**. The prohibited proteins may still be used in other animal feed, including pet food and feed for swine and horses.

People do not get mad cow disease, but scientists have found a link between this disease and a rare brain condition that affects people called variant Creutzfeldt-Jakob disease (vCJD). Researchers believe that people who eat beef from cows infected with mad cow disease are at risk of developing vCJD, which is caused by an abnormal protein in

"NO THANKS—I'M A VEGAN"

Vegans are people who do not eat meat or any animal product such as milk or eggs. They may have become vegans because they would rather not eat animals or because they believe vegan diets are healthier. A vegan diet is totally **vegetarian**; it consists solely of fruits, vegetables, beans, grains, seeds, and nuts. Vegan diets need to be carefully planned to include the essential nutrients humans need to stay healthy. If the diet contains too many **calories** or too few important nutrients, it can be unhealthy.

There are other kinds of vegetarian diets: One includes cheese and other dairy products along with plant foods, and another includes eggs. Still others permit chicken and fish, though not red meat.

the brain called a **prion**. Cells in infected people's brains die until their brains have a spongelike appearance. Like the cows, infected humans lose control of their mental and physical abilities.

Is Medical Testing Necessary?

Animal rights advocates contend that medical-testing projects that use animals are needlessly cruel and old-fashioned and can cause their subjects much pain. Furthermore, they say medical testing on nonhuman species can produce misleading results. Besides, changing the conditions that lead to a disease, not curing or preventing it by using technologies that change the disease itself, is probably better in the long run. Money spent on experiments using animals could instead be spent on preventive measures that might save many more lives. In support of this view, they point out that in many cases researchers choose species less for their similarity to humans and more because they are cheaper and easier to work with and are in many instances familiar to laboratory staff.

Animal-to-Human Transplants

Xenotransplantation carries many risks, not only for the human who receives the **xenograft** but also for the general population. Jonathan Hughes, currently a senior lecturer in ethics at Keele University, North Staffordshire, England, commented on the ethical issues involved in transplanting animal organs into humans: "The most important [ethical] issues here are the risk that diseases transmitted from animals to humans may prove infectious between humans. . . ."

Hughes says that these diseases may lead to new AIDS-type epidemics and costs borne by other patients if resources are moved from other types of medical research to finance xenotransplantation.

If this happens, says Hughes, it takes the ethics of xenotransplantation out of the realm of individual consent and into the realm of *justice*. For example, just how permissible is it for one person to put others at risk for his or her own benefit? The risk of a major new epidemic is extremely grave, and its likelihood is difficult if not impossible to quantify.

If a disease has been transmitted from animals to humans who underwent xenotransplantation, how would the disease be transmitted to other people? Would those who received transplants need to be isolated? Would the disease be airborne, transmitted by touch, coughing, sneezing, or other means? How would the disease be controlled and, ultimately, eliminated? Many believe that xenotransplantations should be stopped until other methods of obtaining human organs have been explored and plans for controlling and preventing transmitted infections can be put in place.

Animal Rights Groups as Advocates and Defenders

There are animal rights groups throughout the world who fight every day to save animals from abuse, find them loving homes, improve the conditions in which they live and may work, and protect and defend their interests in many different ways. One of those ways is through a country's legal system. Over the years, the field of animal law has been growing in many countries. In the United States, attorneys active in shaping this new field founded the Animal Legal Defense Fund (ALDF) in 1979. Their work is supported by hundreds of dedicated attorneys and more than 100,000 members.

> **DID YOU KNOW?**
>
> **"Source animals cannot be freed from all infectious organisms. . . . [I]t may be possible to identify any infectious organism transmitted by xenografting only if it causes disease in humans, and after it has started to do so. . . ."**
>
> **—1997 Nuffield Council Report on Bioethics and the Health Department**

Their work includes the following:

- Filing lawsuits to stop animal abuse and expand the boundaries of animal law.
- Providing free legal assistance to prosecutors handling cruelty cases.

- Working to strengthen state anticruelty statutes.
- Encouraging the federal government to enforce existing animal-protection laws.
- Building the future of animal law through Student Animal Legal Defense Fund chapters and the ALDF's Animal Law Program.
- Providing public education through seminars, workshops, and other outreach efforts.

The ALDF headquarters are located in the San Francisco Bay Area, and another office is located in Portland, Oregon. "Animals are not ours to eat, wear, experiment on, or use for entertainment" is the ALDF slogan.

PETA activists confined themselves in a cage outside a KFC (Kentucky Fried Chicken) restaurant to protest KFC's refusal to adopt basic animal welfare standards.

People for the Ethical Treatment of Animals (PETA) was founded in 1980 by its international president, Ingrid Newkirk, and animal rights activist Alex Pacheco. PETA objects to all mistreatment of animals, but it focuses on ending the use of animals in research labs, in the fur industry, in sports and entertainment, and on factory farms. PETA uses consumer boycotts, lawsuits, protests, educational activities, and undercover investigations. The organization has occasionally sparked criticism for its media stunts and confrontational protests.

There are hundreds of animal rights groups all around the world. Without resorting to violence, their members are working to protect animals and ensure them a healthy, happy life. Among these groups are Animal Activism (Queensland, Australia), the Humane Society of the United States (Washington, D.C.), the American Society for the Prevention of Cruelty to Animals (New York City), the American Humane Association (Denver), Beirut Animals (Lebanon), and the Royal Society for Prevention of Cruelty to Animals (the United Kingdom).

DID YOU KNOW?

While serving in Russia, Henry Bergh, an American diplomat, saw a man whipping his horse. This sight so deeply affected him that when he returned home, he founded the American Society for the Prevention of Cruelty to Animals (ASPCA) in 1866.

Circuses: More Fun for People than Animals?

Lions, tigers, elephants, and bears are among the star performers in circuses. Some people believe that circus life is no life for these animals, which were born to run free in the wild. As a circus travels from place to place, the animals must live and travel in cramped wagons or other vehicles. Often they eat, sleep, and even relieve themselves in the same small space. In some locations, water may be limited; so bathing the animals and cleaning their quarters is limited, as is their supply of drinking water. Elephants' feet are often chained down for long periods, and baby elephants are taken from their mothers for early training. Animals may be exposed to extreme heat or cold. Sometimes they are underfed in order to improve their performances. Disease often breaks out, but veterinarians who treat exotic animals are not always available.

The tricks the circus animals do may amaze and delight audiences, but the ways animals are trained to do them can be cruel. Elephant trainers often drive a bullhook—a rod with a sharp, pointed steel hook on one end—into sensitive areas of an elephant to get the animal to obey commands. Trainers also may use electric shock, whips, baseball bats, and pipes to force animals to cooperate. Some animals are drugged, and others are muzzled to prevent them from defending themselves.

Cruel treatment has resulted in many attacks on humans by animals in distress. In 1994, after a circus elephant killed a trainer in Honolulu, the city introduced a law banning all circuses and other traveling shows from bringing wild animals into Honolulu city or county. In 1995, New Hampshire introduced a bill that would have banned the use of all wild animals in circuses. Neither of the bills passed into law.

DID YOU KNOW?

In Italy, animals cannot be used on television in any way that goes against their nature or subjects them to stress.

BULLFIGHTING: ART OR CRUELTY?

Bullfighting was common in ancient Crete, Thessaly (a region of Greece), and Rome. It is still popular today in Spain, Portugal, southern France, and Latin America. The traditional spectacle has as many as six bullfights. The matador brandishes his cape with skill and grace to draw the bull close to him while avoiding being gored by its horns, and horsemen called picadors then jab the bull with lances to weaken its neck and shoulder muscles. In the final ceremony, the matador performs a ritual slaying of the bull using his sword.

Animal rights advocates call bullfighting a cruel blood sport, but its fans see it as a traditional fine art form that is an important part of Spanish culture. Conchita Citrón, the most famous and respected female bullfighter of modern times, described the bullring as a symbol of different aspects of the world: "Within its small circle one finds life, death, ambition, despair, success, failure, faith, desperation, valor, cowardliness, generosity, and meanness—all condensed into the actions of a single afternoon or even a single moment."

On July 28, 2010, the Spanish region of Catalonia banned bullfighting. Before the vote, animal rights activists had mounted a strong campaign. Some saw the vote as a "message" from a region that strongly supports political and cultural independence from Madrid.

Spanish matador Manuel Jesús "El Cid" makes a pass to a bull during a bullfight at the famous bullring Las Ventas, in Madrid.

Countries around the world that have banned or restricted the use of animals in entertainment include Sweden, Austria, Costa Rica, India, Finland, and Singapore.

WHAT DO YOU THINK?

Do you think animals express emotions? How?

Can you think of any emotions that Darwin left off his list?

Is medical testing using animals necessary?

Would you attend a bullfight or a circus that had wild animal acts? Why or why not?

What are some laws in your community that protect animals?

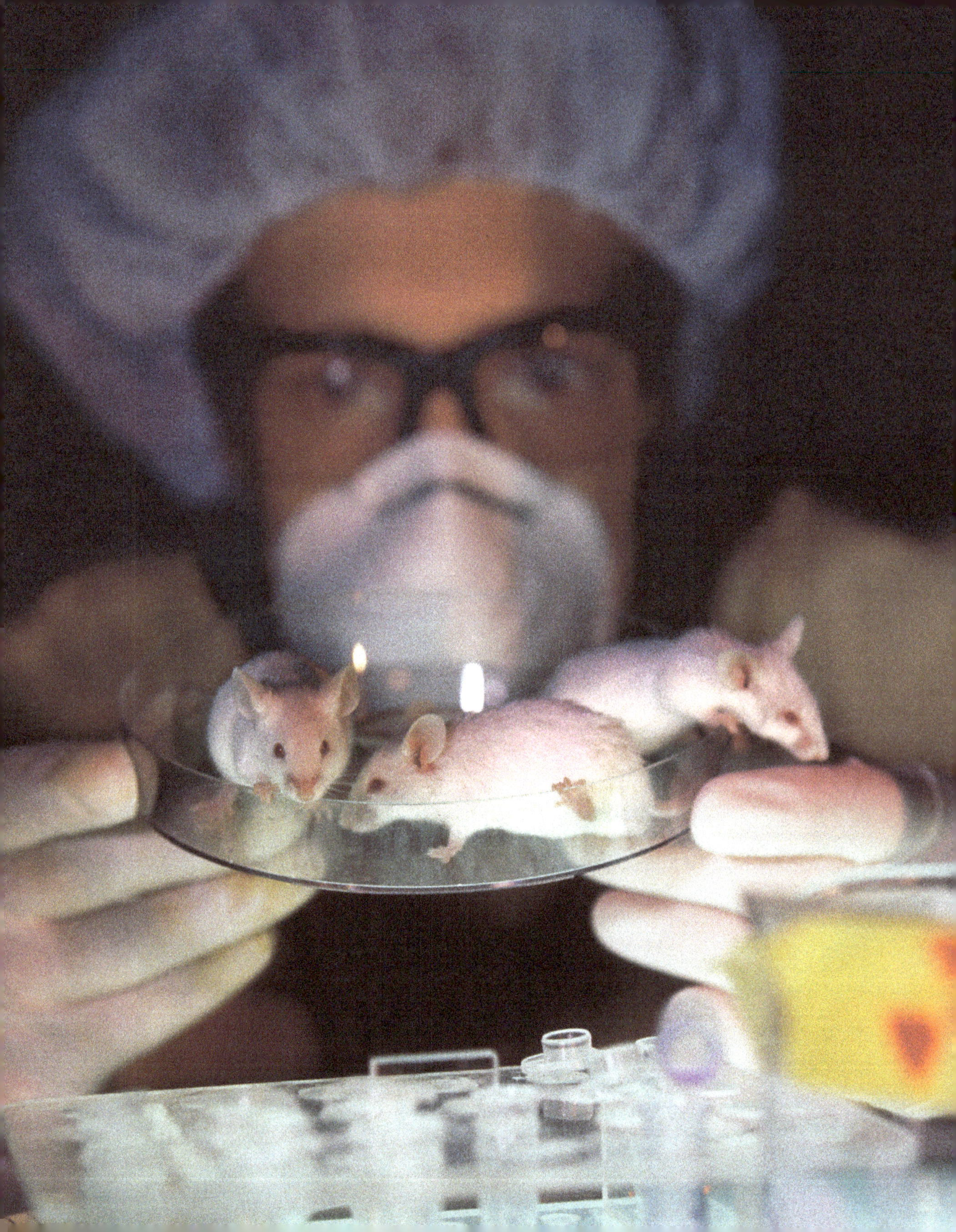

Chapter 4

At the local, regional, and national levels, issues that divide researchers and animal advocates are being debated. Legislation that reflects recent research and the growing interest in animal rights has been passed or proposed. The goal of these new acts and proposals is protection of the interests of animals.

In 2011, after long years of debate, the U.S. Food and Drug Administration was preparing to issue new guidelines on the prolonged use of antibiotics in healthy animals. This use has been blamed for creating resistance to these antibiotic medications in humans. Livestock farmers who oppose the guidelines say there is no proof of a direct link between the farms and human sickness. On the other side are the many scientific groups who are demanding even stronger rules. Among them are the American Medical Association, the Infectious Diseases Society of America, and many others. Dr. Thomas R. Frieden, the director of the CDC, wrote to Congress and cited "compelling evidence" of a "clear link between antibiotic use in animals and antibiotic resistance in humans."

In 2007, the European Union (EU) adopted a directive that improved controls on the use of animals in experiments. The directive includes a

A scientist tests a drug on mice.

ban on using primates such as gorillas, chimpanzees, and orangutans, all of which are threatened with extinction. Other primates included in the ban are macaques, marmosets, vervets, and baboons. The goal of the directive is eventually to end all use of primates in experiments. It is based on what advocates call the Three R's principle: *r*eplace, *r*educe, and *r*efine animal testing.

In 2010, the European Parliament approved legislation that revises the new directive to further improve the welfare of animals used in scientific experiments, ensure fair competition for industry, and foster research activities in the European Union. The legislation is the result of an agreement between the European Parliament and the European

Scientists often use monkeys like this one for testing new drugs and other products.

Council. The revision will make ethical evaluation compulsory and require that experiments using animals be authorized. Other revisions clarify requirements for replacing animals with nonanimal methods and improvements in procedures that will eliminate or reduce to a minimum any possible pain, suffering, distress, or lasting harm to animals. The revised directive includes new oversight measures, such as unannounced inspections. Its goal is to promote research and competitiveness while ensuring that animal welfare is upheld. The new directive will take effect on January 1, 2013.

In 2010, Illinois amended a law that lists dangerous animals to include primates. The state now prohibits ownership or possession of primates; exceptions include zoos, circuses, and colleges. The law also states that those persons who possessed a primate before January 1, 2011, may keep it if the animal is registered. Massachusetts became the first state to make dog or cat devocalization surgery (cutting the animal's vocal chords) a criminal offense.

The Animal Rights Debate

Although people have been learning to understand how and why animals behave the way they do, animals are still used in ways that have created much controversy. In 1975, Peter Singer's book, *Animal Liberation,* shocked readers throughout the world with its description of the abuses of animals in medical experiments and on factory farms. The book inspired a worldwide movement that changed the way humans treat animals. It is now known that animals suffer pain and can express emotions such as joy, grief, and fear. On this basis, some animal activists have acted in lawful and sometimes unlawful ways to secure what they consider animal rights.

On the other side are scientists and others who believe that animal research and scientific testing is an essential tool in the protection of humans from life-threatening diseases. In their view, animal research and testing are not inherently cruel. They hold to the traditional belief that "animal rights" as such do not exist; rather, that human beings have a moral obligation to treat animals with respect and to do them no harm beyond what is necessary to preserve and support human life. That is to say, in terms of animal welfare, people must treat animals humanely, even though sometimes the animals may have to endure pain and suffering from necessary laboratory experiments.

Alternatives Research

A new option has been slowly developing: alternatives research. This is a search for replacements that will reduce the use of animals by means of a step-by-step process. Eventually, its supporters say, the process could lead to elimination of the need for animals. The Johns Hopkins Center for Alternatives to Animal Testing has received grants and gifts to sponsor research, and scientific interest in alternatives has produced legislative initiatives. First, however, researchers must find alternatives that work. The FDA notes that many procedures that could replace animals are still in development. Ultimately, the FDA says, testing must progress to the use of an animal—not using animals for testing would put humans at unreasonable risk. The National Association for Biomedical Research (NABR) contends that in many areas of biologic and medical research, there are no substitutes for the study of living animals. The NABR says many processes in the human body are too complex for computers or cell cultures.

Where do you stand on the animal rights debate? Should animals

A student examines a frog on a virtual frog dissection display at "Frogs: A Chorus of Colors," a 2004 exhibition at the American Museum of Natural History in New York City.

have rights? Perhaps you will want to have a discussion in class, with your friends, or at home. Perhaps you will want to write a story or poem or explore this topic further. What is right? What is wrong? Why? Armed with facts, you can choose your side and argue effectively.

WHAT DO YOU THINK?

This book presents two sides of a controversial issue. Have you taken a side?

Do you think people should regard animals as equals? Why or why not?

Has this book changed the way you think about animals? How?

Do different societies treat animals appropriately? How does your society treat animals?

What is the difference between animal rights and animal welfare?

Glossary

activist—A person who takes strong, direct action that supports one side or another of an issue that has opposing views.

anesthetize—To cause loss of feeling or sensation with or without loss of consciousness.

bearbaiting—The ancient practice of setting dogs upon a chained bear.

calorie—A unit of measure for the amount of heat energy contained in food.

clinical trial—A controlled study of the effectiveness of a drug or medical treatment on test subjects.

cognitive ethology—The study of animal thought and reasoning processes.

compassion—Sympathy for others' distress.

coronavirus—A group of viruses known to pass disease from animals to humans.

cross-contamination—Movement of harmful bacteria from one object, person, or place to another.

Diabecell implants—Type 1 diabetes destroys human insulin-producing cells. The implant is an injection of cells from a pig's pancreas. The pig cells are coated in a seaweed-based gel and release insulin very similar to human insulin.

euthanize—To end a life in a virtually painless way in order to release an animal from incurable disease or severe suffering.

incubate—Maintain in a condition favorable for development.

mucous membrane—A membrane that contains mucous glands.

mutate—To undergo a change.

prion—An abnormal protein particle that lacks nucleic acid and is linked to neurodegenerative diseases.

ruminants—Hoofed animals.

species—In biology, the level of classification below which no further biological distinction can be made. Members of a species share many biological characteristics and can breed with one another.

ultraviolet radiation—One of several kinds of electromagnetic waves that travel through space. The other kinds are radio waves, microwaves, infrared, visible light, X-rays, and gamma rays.

vegetarian—A vegetarian diet is plant-based only, without inclusion of dairy products, eggs, or meats. Some vegetarians also do not eat by-products of animal slaughter such as animal-derived gelatin, cheese, and other foods.

xenograft—The grafting of tissue from one species to another, completely different species.

xenotransplantation—The transplanting of an organ, tissue, or cells from one species—for example, a pig's heart valve—into the body of another species, such as a human.

X-ray radiation—A form of radiation whose extremely short wavelength makes it more highly energized than ultraviolet radiation.

Find Out More

Books

Hayhurst, Chris. *Animal Testing: The Animal Rights Debate*. New York: The Rosen Publishing Group Incorporated, 2000.

Judson, Karen. *Animal Testing* (Open for Debate). Tarrytown, New York: Marshall Cavendish Corporation, 2006.

Martin, Ann M. *A Dog's Life: Autobiography of a Stray*. New York: Scholastic Press, 2005.

Roth, Ruby. *That's Why We Don't Eat Animals: A Book about Vegans, Vegetarians, and All Living Things*. Berkeley, CA: North Atlantic Books, 2009.

Websites

American Society for the Prevention of Cruelty to Animals: Real Issues

www.aspca.org/aspcakids/real-issues/

The Real Issues column lists articles on animal testing, animal abuse in circuses, fur cruelty, tips on caring for your pets in hot and cold weather, and many other topics.

Dosomething.org: Animal Welfare

www.dosomething.org/whatsyourthing/Animal+Welfare

This site contains information related to animal rights and animal welfare.

Minnesota Department of Health: Prevent Cross-Contamination
www.health.state.mn.us/foodsafety/clean/xcontamination.html
Find tips at this site on how to prevent cross-contamination when food shopping, refrigerating food, and preparing and serving it.

People for the Ethical Treatment of Animals
www.PETAKIDS.com
Articles on abuses at circuses and zoos and other topics on animal abuse. Includes information on vegetarianism and how to support animal shelters. Also contains material protesting dissection in the classroom and opposing circus and zoo trips.

Index

Page numbers in boldface are illustrations.

About the Author

Gail Mack is a freelance writer and the author of several books for students. A native of Boston, Massachusetts, she lives and works in New York City.